It Does Matter To Listen
A Collection of Anecdotes

EKPE INYANG

Langaa Research & Publishing CIG
Mankon, Bamenda

Publisher:
Langaa RPCIG
Langaa Research & Publishing Common Initiative Group
P.O. Box 902 Mankon
Bamenda
North West Region
Cameroon
Langaagrp@gmail.com
www.langaa-rpcig.net

Distributed in and outside N. America by African Books Collective
orders@africanbookscollective.com
www.africanbookscollective.com

ISBN-10: 9956-763-58-6

ISBN-13: 978-9956-763-58-0

© Ekpe Inyang 2018

DISCLAIMER
All views expressed in this publication are those of the author and do not
necessarily reflect the views of Langaa RPCIG.

Table of Contents

01   **20 May 2013: Hatred is…**

Hatred is a product of stark ignorance fuelled either by devilish jealousy or haunting fear. If only we knew that, "He receives even more pain who inflicts pain, and more happiness who gives happiness."

02   **3 June 2013: Humans, be fair to one another**

Human beings MUST learn to be fair to every other human being. Gaping gaps of any sort brew jealousy which crystalize into hatred which ultimately may spark off rebellions! The world needs PEACE! And peace can be assured only with the closing up of selfish gaps. Wars are no sign for a healthy EARTH.

03   **26 September 2015: Is it true that it is…?**

Easier to instruct than to learn?

Easier to question than to answer?

Easier to propose than to implement?

Easier to criticize than to create?

Easier to copy than to conceive?

Easier to consume than to produce?

Easier to destroy than to construct?

04 **7 June 2016: Trust your eyes, ears, tongue, legs, hands, pen...?**

Do you trust your eyes, what they see for you? Do you trust your ears, what they hear for you? Do you trust your tongue, what it says for you? Do you trust your legs, where they carry you to? Do you trust your hands, what they grab for you? Do you trust your pen, what it writes for you? Do you trust your hear, what it builds up for you?

05 **13 September 2015: Not your physical glamour...**

It is not your physical glamour, or your intellectual, academic, material possessions [...] that matter; it is the content of your character – your sincerity in word and in deed, your measure of love for others, your purity of heart...

06 **26 February 2013: Life is not just about eating...**

Life is not just about eating and drinking and dressing well. It should focus more on sowing and building for a better future

07 **17 March 2013: Life is a...**

Life is a kaleidoscopic enactment of acts and scenes drawn from two mega-drama scripts written at the beginning of time by two opposing playwrights.

08 1992: Not the only predator

Man is not the only predator but his addition to the number is of colossal ecological consequences.

09 20 February 2013: Mind and heart are different

The mind and the heart are two different things; you may have the mind to stand up for something but not the heart to do so.

10 10 June 2013: Life, a narrow path

Life is a narrow path on which we must walk with caution, as there are obvious and subtle distractions and obstacles along the way. Having a clear aim and staying focused are a useful strategy.

11 31 October 2013: One day our nations shall...

One day our nations shall be populated by individuals who share a common mission and vision and who truly and genuinely care about the present and future condition of Mother Earth and humankind by developing and implementing strategies that mend the present scars of marginalisation, exploitation, avarice and greed in order to give humankind the smooth skin of sustainable consumption for balanced and sustainable development as health herbs for Mother Earth.

9 April 2014: Revisiting 1992

12 I remember writing this in my call it conservation album in 1992, for visitors to read when they come visiting. Does it still make sense today?

"Man is not the only predator but his addition to the number is of colossal ecological consequences."

In fact, man's ecological footprints continue to grow larger and larger, and eco-systems are systematically replaced by ego-systems.

What portion of the Earth is still living and what portion is almost dead, if not already dead, cannot be calculated by the most talented mathematicians of our time.

We are like a frog swimming in cold water in a pot on fire, to borrow from Al Gore. The water gets a little warm, and the frog says, "This is terrific." Then the water gets really warm, and the frog says, "Still OK." But then, it gets warmer and warmer, and guess what finally happens to the frog.

We humans are wiser than that frog but seem to have chosen not to be! Even with mounting evidences of drastic changes in biodiversity and global climate, we seem to demand for more proof before make a shift from our current consumption and other behavioural patterns!

13 **9 October 2015: Drama of love**

The drama of love needs no prompter - it happens naturally! And once there is love the stream of things flow like a young river over a smooth terrain - no hills, no valleys. No one can deny that happiness is the fruit of love and peace the seeds that need to be sown for it to grow and grow and grow.

14 **10 October 2015: Success achieved by dubious means**

There is no sustainability in any success achieved by dubious means. In fact, such a result should not be counted as success at all; it is like building a house on a foundation rested on a sandy surface and claiming, or exclaiming, "I have done it!"

15 **24 September 2015: Natural gift for gossiping**

Those with the natural gift for gossiping interpret any voices heard as engaging in back-biting; those with the natural flair for lying regard every single report as embellished with falsehood; those with the natural acumen for stealing see every movement as a strategy for breaking into a house; those with the natural propensity to kill are frightened by their shadows envisioned as enemies bearing swords.

---

16 **26 September 2015: Rubbish in, rubbish out…**

We often say rubbish in, rubbish out - but there are times when you put in stuff and rubbish comes out, especially when someone else has to come out with the finished product!

---

17 **7 March 2013: What the world needs**

The world needs genuine love, unity and mutual respect and support more than ever before, if we must evade Nature's apocalyptic response to human nefarious acts of greed and man's inhumanity to fellow man

---

18 **1 December 2013: Where great rivers meet**

Where great rivers meet there is accumulation of nutrients; when exchange visits are made there is a subtle blending of rich cultures; when sound minds rub there is an improvement and a consolidation of healthy ideas.

19   2 July 2015: The only strategy for sustainability *(In commemoration of WEEC 2015)*

Please, don't laugh - it is the truth...Listen, everybody, listen to me as I speak to you from this rostrum. I had a dream last night...after listening to theories propounded by pundits and learning from examples shared by indefatigably committed practitioners in the fields of conservation, research, technology, education, propaganda...And in that dream I discovered what, for centuries, humanity has been looking for - the secret how to shape (call it twist!) the earth towards sustainability. Now I have the single, most important solution. Now you don't need to waste your precious breath, energy, quality time and other resources organising meetings, traveling long distances to these meetings - spending sleepless nights preparing papers, standing on the podium, delivering these to huge, inquisitive, questioning crowds, talking out your lungs to give further explanations to what you are not really sure will work; or sitting in auditoriums, racking your brain to figure out meanings, straining your eyes to read between the lines, or engaging in debates to share and clarify ideas, ideologies, values and experiences. Simply listen to me, ladies and gentlemen, and do exactly what I say, not what I do. ONLY I KEEP THE SECRET, the simple, single truth, the only strategy for sustainability!!!

20 18 January 2014: You seemed to know your divine mission

You seemed to know your divine mission and had prayed to God that your guess was right. You have developed your implementation strategy and shown this to those around you whose suggestions point to different, opposite routes, as they try to confuse you. But you have received a response from that silent, divine voice to move ahead with your original plans. However, while you should not overtly turn down the suggestions of those around you – which could create a conflict between you and them whose ploy is clearly to lead you to failure – move on in obedience of that divine voice, to achieve that most desired result, that wide-impact outcome that will guide and save humankind! And when this is made manifest, even the distracting voices may openly join you in the celebrations, to share the credit. Thank them for the part they played and, as similar results are recorded in their repeated attempts to lead you to failure, they may, henceforth, secretly work to mend their ways in clear realisation that their collective weapons are too weak to break that single, divine amour that protects you in your divinely approved mission. No one can change your destiny, even though this may be delayed! Such delays even prepare you better for the greater assignment, to the disappointment – and regret – of those that work against you! Criticisms and derailments are simply the reinforcing plates of the divine amours of those charged with great assignments!

<table>
<tr><td>**21**</td><td>**11 May 2016: I learnt from a young Manager**</td></tr>
</table>

I learnt this from a young Cameroonian Manager of a Plant Installation company whom I admired so much as he went about his business, effectively communicating with his staff and a team of consultants, around 7:30 a.m., on his way to his office: "When the issue you want to address is urgent, SIMPLY MAKE A CALL and NOT JUST SEND AN EMAIL. When there is still plenty of time to address the issue, say, A MONTH OR TWO BEFORE implementation, SEND AN EMAIL but remember to FOLLOW UP WITH REGULAR CALLS when the deadline is approaching - A WEEK OR TWO BEFORE implementation, A FEW DAYS BEFORE implementation, and even EARLY ON THE DAY of implementation. There should be NO ASSUMPTION that you have effectively COMMUNICATED BY EMAIL. THE COMMON EXPERIENCE here, even when using the MOBILE TELEPHONE, is that we are OFTEN TOLD: "THE NUMBER YOU ARE CALLING IS NOT AVAILABLE AT THE MOMENT, PLEASE TRY AGAIN LATER', which the EMAIL WILL NOT GIVE as FEEDBACK FOR COMMUNICATION DELAY OR FAILURE."

<table>
<tr><td>**22**</td><td>**13 May 2016: What is not management and what is management**</td></tr>
</table>

Management is not going for nitty-gritties in ways that may discourage personal initiatives or creativity, it is pursuing strategic issues that can support overall success; it is not listening for and encouraging the spread of gossips that can strain staff relationships, it is teasing out and facilitating the spread of ideas that can contribute to their effective collaboration for increased performances; it is not claiming to know everything in the minutest detail unimaginable, it is admitting that there is a lot to learn even from the most junior staff; it is not trying to change everyone to act, behave or have the same views like you, it is supporting everyone to develop their own potentials or philosophies; it is not making yourself appear like a silent competitor over technical issues, it is making yourself seen as an open supporter of technical efforts; it is not only looking for every means to reduce costs, it is also providing adequate resources for regular activity implementation and opportunities for career growth to ensure sustained staff motivation and delivery of quality results; it is not merely focusing on policies and procedures, it is also knowing where and when discretions can be used without violating these; it is not looking for the slightest faults to hurt those you hate for personal or other reasons, it is looking for the smallest good examples to highlight and build a good image for the organisation, institution or company; it is not openly scolding or blaming when mistakes are made, it is privately advising and setting good examples that can be copied for the general good; it is not only about focusing on the technical or professional side of life, it is also about paying attention to the personal or family side of life; it is not only about being fast and smart in making decisions, it is mostly about weighing the facts, the evidences and the circumstances, as well as the possible consequences, before making the decisions; it is not about snootily being discriminatory, nepotistic or vindictive in your dealings with the staff, it is about humbly being objective, open and fair in your relations with them; it is not about being always ready to mete out punishment to those who have gone astray or underperformed, it is about being always ready to find the least opportunity to reward good acts or performances for others to emulate.

18 October 2015: THIEF

| 23 |

Total
Humiliation
Inhabits
Every
Fountain of your life

24   **22 May 2014: Acquire more of education…**

Acquire more of education than knowledge; share more of values than facts; give more of love than material possessions.

13 October 2015: LEADER

25   Love your follower

Encourage your follower

Assist your follower

Defend your follower

Empathise with your follower

Reward your follower

26   **18 March 2016: Sang national anthem backwards**

A talented young was arrested because he was heard singing the national anthem backwards. "No, set him free!" ordered the Police Commissioner. "Instead this rare creativity deserves a national award," he added to the consternation of everyone present at the scene.

26 October 2015: FOLLOWER

27   Find a level ground with your leader

Obviate all possible sources of conflict with your leader

Love your leader

Lower swords with your leader

Organise your actions within the broader organizational context shared with your leader

Withdraw from dialogues that distort the truth needed by your leader

Encourage the development of a positive atmosphere that inspires your leader and other colleagues

Restrain from open confrontation with your leader

25 October 2015: MURDERER

28

Men
Under
Riotous
Demonic
Engulfment
Release
Ecliptic
Rays

17 October 2015: LIER

29

Lower yourself
Into an abyss of
Everlasting
Regrets

30 **2016: Why are we ESDing?**
Because by selling our strategy we guarantee sustainable development.

So join us in our mission of

Ever
Supporting
Development that lasts forever!!!

31 **17 May 2016: Libya and Liberia**

America **A**frica
Must **M**ust
Stop **S**tart
To **T**o
Entertain **E**ncourage
Libya Liberia

32 **8 April 2014: Any other planet?**
Is there any planet better equipped for humans than Earth? This is the single most important question we must constantly ask ourselves as we Mow, Muse, and Move about.

33 **28 February 2013: Education**
Education should not only enrich your head but should nourish your mind, strengthen your heart, and guide your vision and action.

34   2 September 2013: Ever imagined?

Have you ever imagined someone whose official responsibility is to make you succeed in your job turning out to be the one who would be glad to see you fail? How would such a person feel when finally you succeeded after his several rehearsals of your failure?

35   12 March 2014: People of good or bad character…

People of good character are torchlights in the darkest hours of the night everywhere they go. On the contrary, those of bad character are a cloud of darkness in the brightest hours of the day wherever they set their feet. We all have a choice to be either "the good" or "the bad." But remember: "It is good to be good."

36   18 May 2016: I beg your pardon

"I beg your pardon", she said sneeringly and walked off, causing the young man's shoulders droop.

37   9 October 2013: The beauty of Mother Earth

The beauty of Mother Earth is in her green shoes, green skirt, green blouse, green headscarf, green lips and green eyes! To rob her of green is to send her to an ugliness contest!

38 | 10 July 2015: Glad to be safely back

Glad to be safely back in Cameroon after the very interesting World Environmental Education Congress in Gothenburg, the more than interesting tour of Sweden (Haparanda, Sandskar, and even the dashes to nearby Finland, stopping at the Arctic Circle!), and, especially, the terrific hospitality shown to me by colleagues and friends, (indeed, brothers and sisters!) of WWF Sweden. I feel so good after all what I received from them - the warmth and care and love from Germund, Gunilla...; Staffan and Lena and children and grandchildren; Olle and wife and children; Ula and Annissa and children, and Asa and child. I love you all!!! I use this medium to wish you all more and more blessings from God!!! To WWF Sweden, I simply lack the words to express my profound gratitude for making my trip to Sweden possible!!! God bless everyone who has been behind this success, who fought so hard to make me have the opportunity to distract myself from the pain I was then going through!!!

39 | 5 June 2016: No proclamations required

Intellectuals do not require self-proclamations but consistent unintentional, modest and "glocally" appealing verbalisations and actions to be acknowledged as such.

5 September 2013: Drama is…

40

Drama is a re-enactment of real or imagined life events, presented either as hyperbole or "hypobole", served in a fine dish of dialogue and action to facilitate digestion. This explains why you can make an accurate guess how a drama will end not only from the renditions of the characters but more so from their individual and collective actions. And, as a note of caution, we are all actors and actresses on an ever-widening stage of life, watched by an ever-increasing number of "spec-actors", spectators, and "repor-actors".

17 May 2016: Expect no thank you for doing good

41

The people you have shown great love and kindness may pay you back with scorn and hatred. Never always expect thank you for doing good, lest you feel frustrated with life. Simply take doing good for a clear and good purpose as part of your contribution even to the faceless and shameless crop that constitutes an integral part of the humanity that you care for and for the sake of God the God that you serve. And, someday, your reward may come a hundredfold from those you do not even know.

17 May 2016: Millions of fraudulent guys out there

42

There are millions of fraudulent guys out there, in different cloaks and scarfs. But the worst are a set specialised in making the whole world faithfully believe that they are the most trusted.

<table><tr><td>43</td></tr></table>

1992: The best way to understand a people

The best way to understand a people is to live with the people; the best way to live with the people is to share with the people, and the best thing to share with the people is what the people need.

18 May 2016: True son of Africa

<table><tr><td>44</td></tr></table>

Peter promised him a blur**B**
André gave him a bikin**I**
Until he felt like a bo**Y**
Like a true son of Afric**A**

<table><tr><td>45</td></tr></table>

18 May 2016: Cars are fast becoming clothes

The more we get glued to the material things of this world, the more the material things of this world get glued to us. You may be surprised to learn that today some flashy cars are regarded by some hyper-materialistic people in much the same way as we regard the clothes we wear, except that these people have not yet developed muscles strong enough to put these on instead of get into them. Or, perhaps, because the design is not appropriate for this new style of life, these people are already (silently) advocating for a new set of cars designed for putting on rather than getting into before driving around to enjoy life to the fullest.

46 | 18 May 2016: The Cunning Gang and The Group

This time he knew he would be caught red-handed if he didn't act smartly and swiftly. There was a vigilante group coming towards him. He could see their flashlights and hear their footsteps fast approaching.

He took out a whistle from his trousers pocket and started blowing, running and shouting at the same time, "Thief, thief, thief!" Soon the vigilante group joined him, running and shouting all over the place.

Suddenly he stopped, stepped aside and let the vigilante group continue running before he started running in the opposite direction. He went right back to the spot where he had hidden a television set, a laptop computer, a gas bottle and a money safe.

The young lady met him there and said, "That was so smart of you."

"You are simply fabulous, my angel," said the young man. "You were able to text me the right time to come around, opened the back door carefully for me and went back in and slept as if you were not part of the deal."

"It is a role I could not afford not to have performed, Daddy."

"Now give yourself just a month before you leave that house and join me. We need to bring up our son together."

"The man thought I was there just for that little money. I suspect he was even taking me for a fool. Because I pretended not to be the talking type, not to be the knowing type, but to be that innocent little baby. Now I have increased the pay a hundred times."

"The power of silence! The power of acting foolishly for a purpose! You played your part so well, honey. Mwah! Honestly, we have taken quite enough to start our own life.

"Enough, indeed, Daddy. We are so lucky, so blessed! The man has been trusting me so blindly. Anyway, 'you need to trust the person who takes care of your baby', hahaha!"

"Now you have to make him really believe that your father is so sick that he needs you home urgently to take care of him."

"But he called dad the other day – right in my presence – and dad almost betrayed me. Daddy is such a fool, you know. Always bent on speaking the truth. I was so embarrassed."

"Never mind, I will give you some more tips how to go about it…I better hurry out of here before The Group turns right back, disappointed at not finding any trace of the thief over there."

"The Group has met with The Cunning Gang. They seem not to use their brains the way they use their flashlights and machetes and guns…Bye, Daddy."

She sneaked back into the house, leaving the backdoor wide open in order not to raise any suspicion. Her roommates were still fast asleep. She lay on her bed and exchanged more text messages with her fiancé for about thirty minutes before sleeping. Evidently, it was all about how she should conduct herself in the morning when the news would have broken out.

"Concentrate on taking care of the baby so you don't have to give any explanations…Simply tell them you could not remember the last person who used the back door…No, no, no, avoid going towards that door so you don't inadvertently act out what you did and raise suspicion…"

47 | 22 May 2016: Optimism

Optimism is the only magic when success seems either far-fetched or uncertain. Encapsulated in an attitude of cheerfulness, optimism is an antidote against the stress or some other form of emotional disturbance that would have weighed you down and caused you to fail.

48 | 22 May 2016: Love may sometimes hurt children

Children are the extensions and integral parts of their parents who naturally feel or supply their warmth. No one can worry about the children more than their parents; no one can labour for the children more than their parents; no one can care for the children more than their parents; and no one can love the children more than their parents. Parents (teenage, physically handicapped, insane) have a natural propensity—call it an irresistible response to the genetic command—to nourish and nurture their children (adult, stubborn, invalid)! But sometimes the love and care shown can be so strong that these may instead hurt the children. This means that parents must know the doses of love and care to give to their children for positive results.

49 | 22 May 2014: The Illiterate wife

There was a professor that got married to a very beautify but illiterate lady. The couple had just concluded their honeymoon, and there was a party to commemorate this.

The professor was to make an elaborate speech in praise of his beautiful wife, recounting how it all started and sharing some of the interesting, though not secret, part of their honeymoon experiences.

The lady's role was to welcome the guests with: "We are happy to welcome you to our party." This sentence was rehearsed several timed before the guests started arriving.

The first set of guests arrived: "We are happy to welcome you to our party."

After about thirty minutes, the second set arrived: "We are happy to party you to our welcome."

In another thirty minutes, the third set arrived: "We are party to welcome you to our happy."

The professor could not hide his embarrassment, and guess what happened. "Ladies and gentlemen, the party is postponed until further notice."

No one seemed to have understood what had been said and sat glued to their seats, looking at the assorted dishes and drinks set on three tables in front of them.

Apparently, no one had even noticed that the lady had been fumbling so badly with the welcome sentence, particularly since she spoke in some foreign accent that must have easily passed for American English.

23 May 2016: Beware what you imitate!

50

Imitating how people dance or sing can make you a good or a bad dancer or singer. If a good dancer or singer, you will undoubtedly receive cheers and even earn an income. If a bad dancer or singer, you will unsurprisingly receive jeers. But you can give the bad dancing or singing a comic twist and attract cheers and earn an income for being a good comedian. But imitating how people talk and what they say may land you in serious trouble. So beware what you imitate!

23 May 2016: No matter how you try to transform

Being the child of a farmer may not necessarily make you a farmer; being the child of a hunter may not necessarily make you a hunter; being the child of a teacher may not necessarily make you a teacher; being the child of a medical doctor may not necessarily make you a medical doctor; being the child of a successful person may not necessarily make you a successful person; being the child of an unsuccessful person may not necessarily make you an unsuccessful person; being the child of a particular country may not necessarily make you remain a citizen of that country; but being the child of a particular race will always make you remain a descendant of that race…no matter how much you try to transform your physiological, psychological, or metaphysical character.

26 May 2016: Certainly not for the feeble-minded

Leadership is not for the feeble-minded; it is not for the over-bearing; it is not for the indecisive and confused; it is not for the self-opinionated; it is not for the short-sighted; it is not for the over-ambitious; it is not for the self-centred; it is not for the over-generous; it is not for the grudge-laden and vengeful; it is not for the callous and cold-hearted; it is not for the over-compassionate; it is simply for those with an unwavering and clear vision, a genuine passion and a relentless commitment for the good of all.

53 31 May 2014: Alpha Blondy, a genuine intellectual

Alpha Blondy is a genuine intellectual with a soft heart for humanity. His ability to control the emotions of the audience during his performances, creating such a powerful atmosphere of empathy and love, is what strikes me the most about this great man of Ivory Coast. He is, undoubtedly, the greatest artist in Ivory Coast and one of the greatest in Africa and the world at large.

54 4 June 2016: Fear of disease and death

It is the fear of disease and of death and the eerie atmosphere of inevitability and unpredictability that surround these two most dreaded earthly phenomena that have humbled and scarred the cantankerous regiment of dictatorial and oppressive humans and, as a result, protected millions of the gullible and vulnerable crop from the bleeding swords of their unparalleled whims and caprices.

55 5 June 2016: The cunning lot

The cunning lot represents a few most unsuspected individuals who stab in the backyard and closed rooms and praise in the front yard and conference rooms, thus giving the impression that they are supportive of the disdainful actions of their colleagues or bosses, "friends" or relatives in order to continue to win their protection or support.

56 | 5 June 2016: Three reasons why people lie

The world is full of moments of ups and downs, of undue burdens and responsibilities, of jealousies and envies, of wicked intentions and actions, and of rivalries and power struggles, which often drives some people to tell ludicrous and hurtful lies. Here are three reasons why such people tell lies:

i) To get themselves out of humiliating, costly or dangerous situations that would have otherwise made them lose their respect, positions, money, properties or lives, or unduly increase their load-work, burdens or responsibilities;

ii) To reduce perceived pressures of competition from those seen as strong rivals by slyly concealing their deficiencies and failures as well as the potentials and achievements of others, and by furtively presenting themselves as the only ones competent enough to handle certain tasks and assignments so as to take advantage of certain opportunities, and

iii) To be seen as the only nice and loyal ones ever by painting others as the most disrespectful, disloyal and temperamental so as to win the support and favour of those in stronger or superior positions.

|57| **5 June 2016: What have been my contributions?**

At a particular age and/or in particular circumstances, it is honest and prudent to pause and critically ask yourself the hard question: "What have been my contributions, at home or in my workplace, to deserve the sumptuous daily meals, the high daily, weekly or monthly pocket allowances or wages, or the exuberant annual recognitions or rewards?" Remember, anyone with the habit of free-riding or who relies on the generosity of free lunch may end up being the extremely lazy, starving or misfortune-prone type. If found in such a generous situation against your will, it is logical and expedient to reflect on, or find out, why you get such steady benefits without your contributing anything; such things may not always come by the grace of God to prosper you but could also signify the bait of a god to possess, control and eventually destroy you.

|58| **5 June 2016: You can't destroy or hide a star**

There are no tongues of fire, no matter how strong, that can so easily burn off a star that is in itself bonfire and there is no depth of darkness that can succeed in swallowing up and hiding it from being noticed when its rays are capable of dissipating the most impenetrable clouds of darkness. By the same token, it is a sheer waste of effort to try to kill someone destined for great achievements, who has just begun his or her journey towards greatness and it is silly to try to hide a high-intensity lamp under the table at a great nightly ceremony for recognising awesome sources of light.

59 5 June 2016: Eradicating racism (*Inspired by and in memory of Muhammad Ali whose other side of the greatness I had just discovered*)

Tremendous effort has been made to reduce racism in most societies and countries on this earth, with the resultant rapid increase in inter-racial respect, inter-racial trust, inter-racial cooperation and inter-racial marriages...But to completely eradicate this negative trait, it may require, inter alia, banning the use of all forms of linguistic inventions associated with it: blackleg, black sheep, black cat, blackmail, black book, black man, black history, black culture; nigger, slave, slavery; monkey, primitive, uncivilized, civilized; inferior, superior, developed, under developed, Third World, North and South, The West, the rest of the world; tribe, tribesman, tribal, tribalism; white man, white house, white paper, white culture; colonial master, oyibo, colonialism, neo-colonialism...The list is so, so long! Let the youth take this as a challenge, to make the world a better place!

60 5 June 2016: A talent doesn't rely on human pity

A talent doesn't rely on human pity,

favour or benevolence to succeed; a combination of his or her well-defined vision, unrivalled prowess, undying energy, relentless determination, indefatigably positive nature, sincere humility, loving kindness, invigorating and inspiring sense of humour, unreservedly honest, unique and healing message to mankind, unconditional magnanimity to the poor, down-to-earth attitude and respect towards fans and reverential fear of God is enough to attract that much-need divine favour that will, despite perceived delays, eventually catapult him or her to his or her most destined level of achievement.

61   6 June 2016: That small inner voice

In you there are two voices: the first is urging you to go left and the second is imploring you to take right. The first is so strong, imposing and seemingly convincing. The second is so soft, small and seemingly unpersuasive. The first seems to surround you like a storm, banging on the cords of your carelessness and impulsiveness. The second seems to come from within you like a breeze, playing on the cords of your consciousness and conscience. The first tells you how successful you will be if you follow that plan to the letter. The second warns you to pause and ponder on the plan. The first warns that the opportunity will be lost if you continue to procrastinate. The second reminds you of the saying, "Think before you act." The first considers you as indecisive and phlegmatic. The second feels it is prudent to appear irrational and absurd by always giving it a second thought.

| 62 | **7 June 2016: Style, path and stance** |

You may choose to adopt a style that is simple but never consider one that is simplistic; you may choose the highly creative path but never consider one that is absurd; you may take a critical stance in your approach but never consider one that is insolent.

| 63 | **7 June 2016: Sharing not by shredding or shearing** |

It is nice to be seen out there sharing but this should not be done by shredding or shearing.

| 64 | **10 June 2016: Farewell, Muhammad Ali** |

Farewell, Muhammad Ali. I knew you as the greatest boxer when I was a boy but as a man I discovered you were the greatest beyond the boxing ring, impacting the young and the old in all corners of the world. You have defeated death by your multitalented skills in boxing, charming sense of humour in oratory and poetry, boundless love for humanity in your subtle fight to break the walls of racism, and extraordinary charisma that inspires and empowers the poorest, the powerless and most marginalised in society.

65. 11 June, 2016: Beware your debtors!

Most of your debtors were your friends only at the time when you had just given them the loans. But, take note, the friendship might be far, far gone with most of them, now that the debts are so, so old and they are unable or unwilling to pay back. Have you ever noticed that each time you showed up where some of your debtors were, they felt so, so embarrassed? You are now such a source of discomfiture in the lives, particularly, of those unable to pay their debts that they wish you were no longer living [near] where they stay, if not dead, so they can regain the peace of mind they need to live their normal lives once again. So beware your debtors!

6 January, 2017: Good to work hard daily, wise to rest well nightly

It is good to work hard daily but also wise to rest well nightly if daily you must work hard again and again.

66. 23 January, 2016: Never mind what is said about you

Never mind what is said about you that may sound ugly. If it is the wrong image that is painted, this can never change the real you. But if it is the right image that is portrayed, then you need to work on your character sooner rather than later.

67 15 February, 2016: The beauty of a human

The beauty of a human should not be judged only by what is seen on the outside but by what is packaged deep in the heart in the form of peace, love, kindness and care.

www.ingramcontent.com/pod-product-compliance
Lightning Source LLC
Chambersburg PA
CBHW021550270326
41930CB00008B/1445